Ben Parker

EASY
UKULELE
TUNES

30 Fun and Easy Ukulele Tunes for Beginners

Author: Ben Parker

Editor: Alison McNicol

First published in 2014 by Kyle Craig Publishing

This version updated Dec 2014

Text and illustration copyright © 2014 Kyle Craig Publishing

Design and illustration: Julie Anson

Music set by Ben Parker using Sibelius software

ISBN: 978-1-908707-37-6

A CIP record for this book is available from the British Library.

A Kyle Craig Publication

www.kyle-craig.com

Contents

Humpty Dumpty

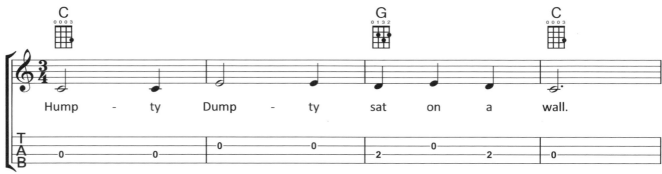

Hump - ty Dump - ty sat on a wall.

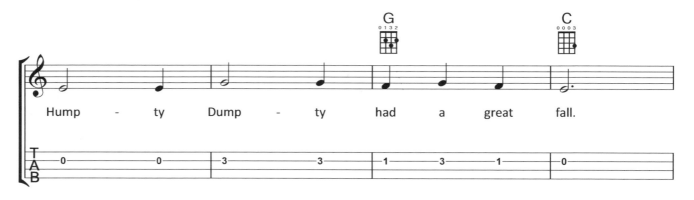

Hump - ty Dump - ty had a great fall.

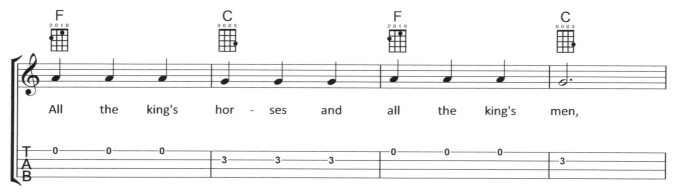

All the king's hor - ses and all the king's men,

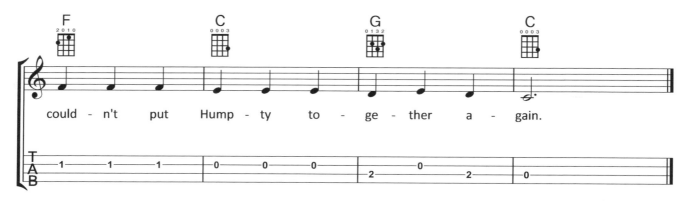

could - n't put Hump - ty to - ge - ther a - gain.

Oh When The Saints

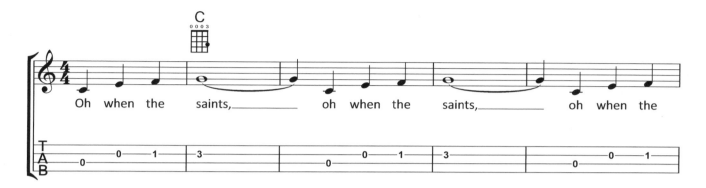

Oh when the saints,_____ oh when the saints,_____ oh when the

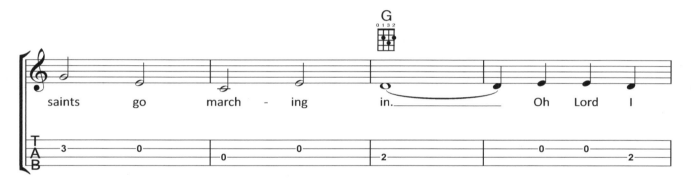

saints go march - ing in._____ Oh Lord I

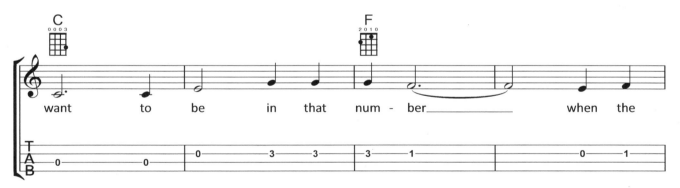

want to be in that num - ber_____ when the

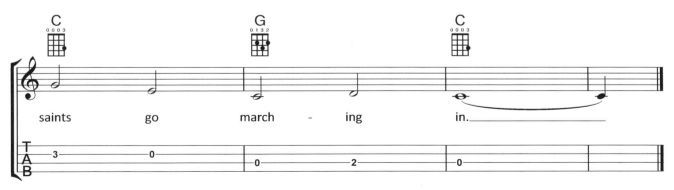

saints go march - ing in._____

The Grand Old Duke Of York

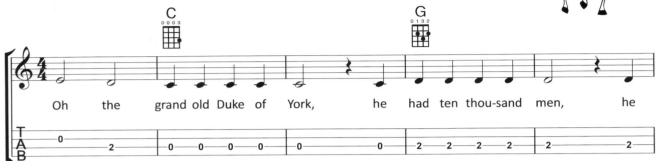

Oh the grand old Duke of York, he had ten thou-sand men, he

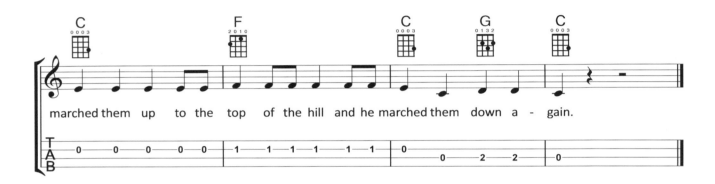

marched them up to the top of the hill and he marched them down a - gain.

Skip To My Lou

Skip, skip, skip to my Lou. Skip, skip, skip to my Lou.

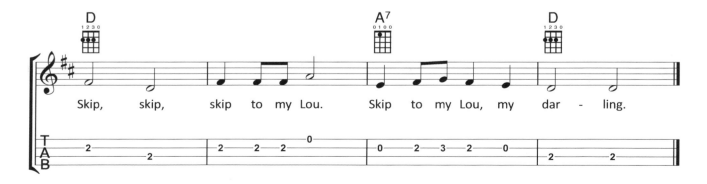

Skip, skip, skip to my Lou. Skip to my Lou, my dar - ling.

Oranges And Lemons

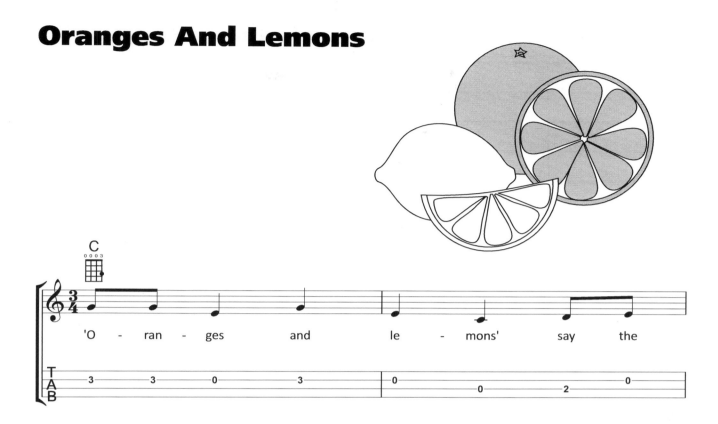

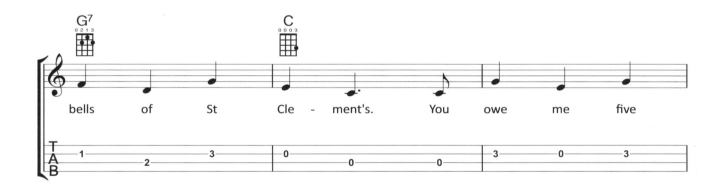

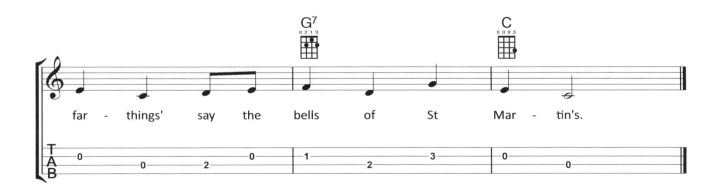

My Old Man

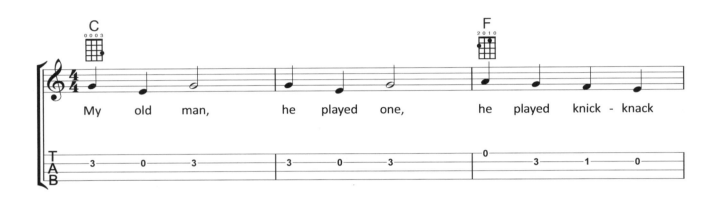

My old man, he played one, he played knick - knack

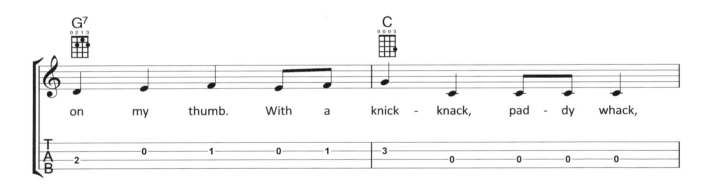

on my thumb. With a knick - knack, pad - dy whack,

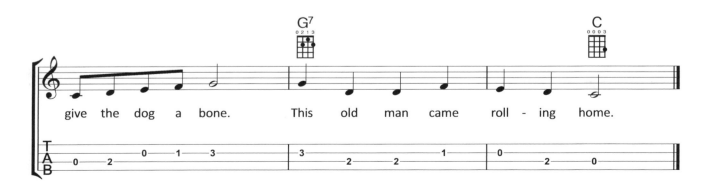

give the dog a bone. This old man came roll - ing home.

Scotland The Brave

Home On The Range

Oh, give me a home where the buf - fa - lo roam, where the

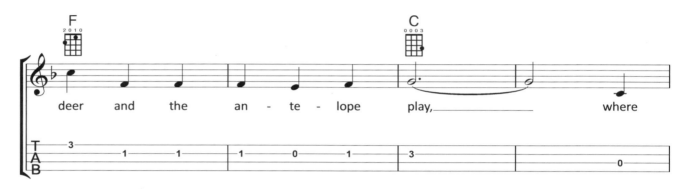

deer and the an - te - lope play, _____ where

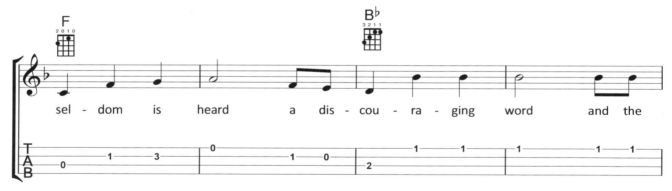

sel - dom is heard a dis - cou - ra - ging word and the

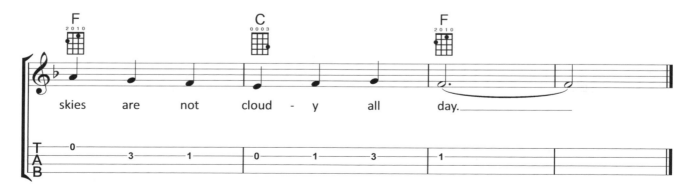

skies are not cloud - y all day. _____

Old MacDonald

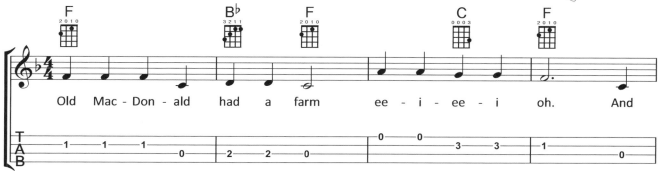

Old Mac-Don - ald had a farm ee - i - ee - i oh. And

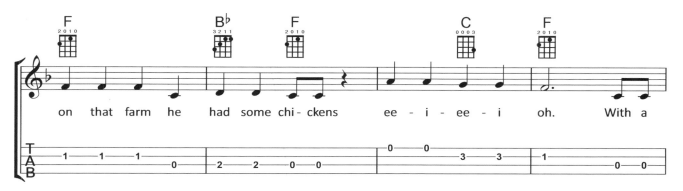

on that farm he had some chi - ckens ee - i - ee - i oh. With a

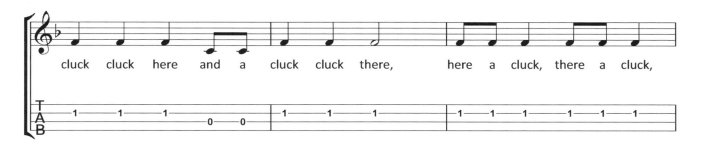

cluck cluck here and a cluck cluck there, here a cluck, there a cluck,

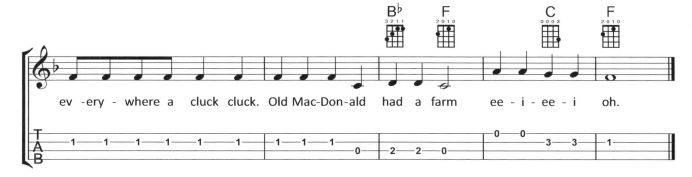

ev -ery - where a cluck cluck. Old Mac-Don-ald had a farm ee - i - ee - i oh.

Comin' Round The Mountain

Hush Little Baby

Clementine

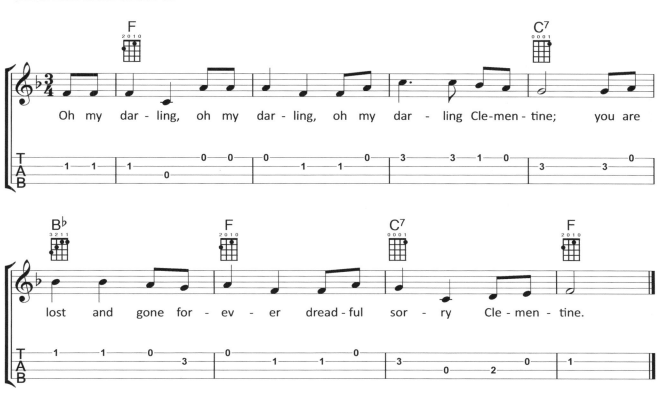

Song Of The Volga Boatmen

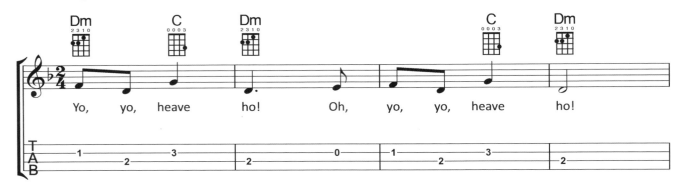

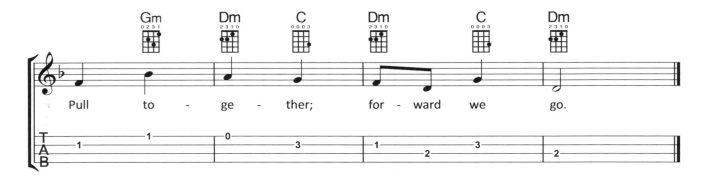

Dear Liza

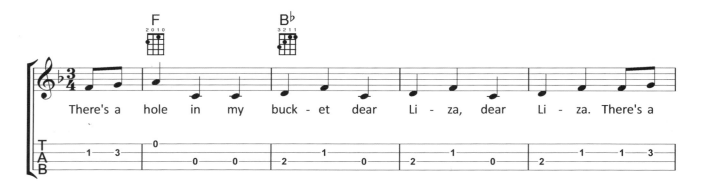

Amazing Grace

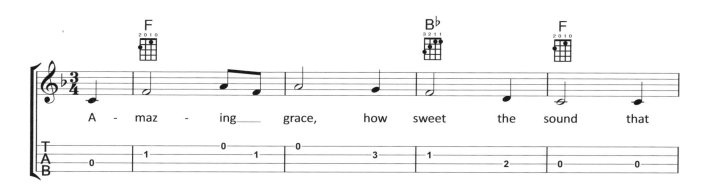

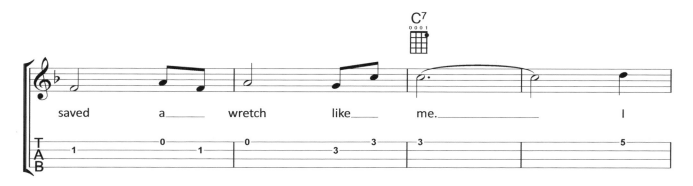

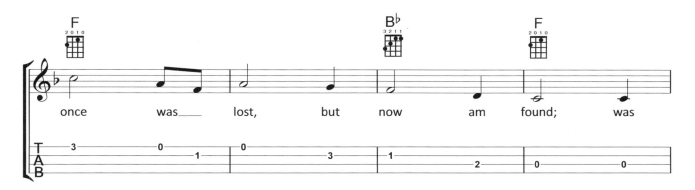

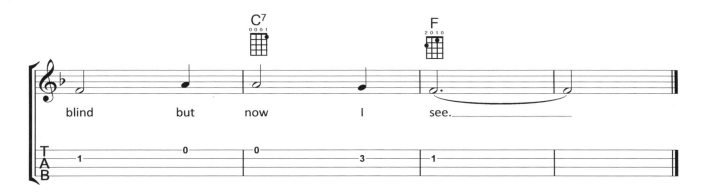

My Bonnie

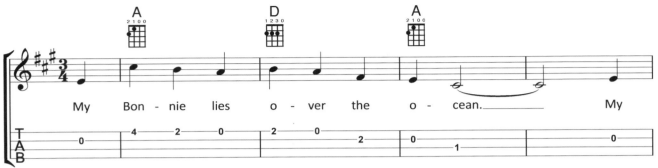

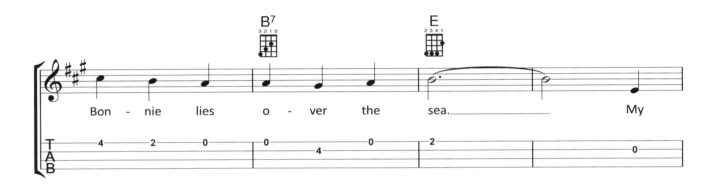

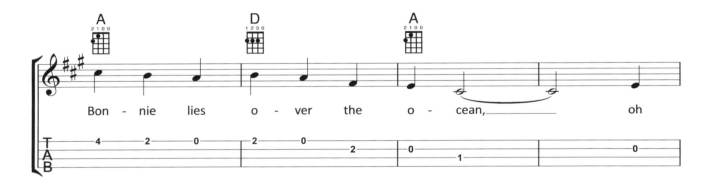

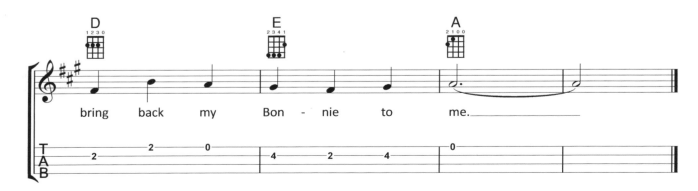

I Saw Three Ships

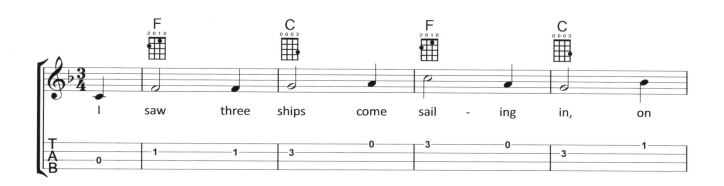

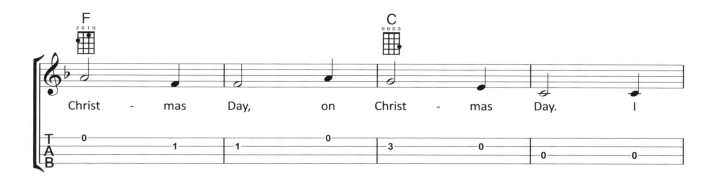

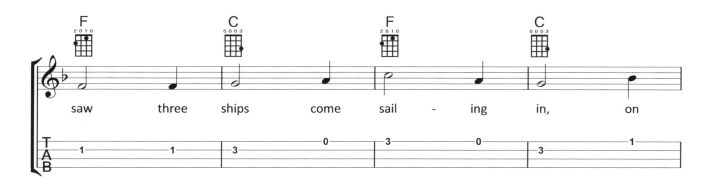

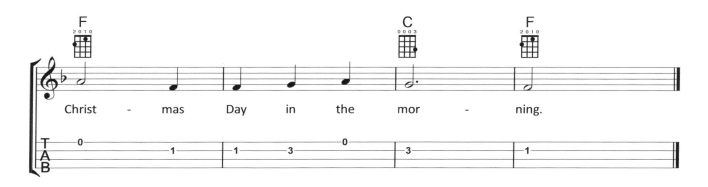

Au Clare De La Lune

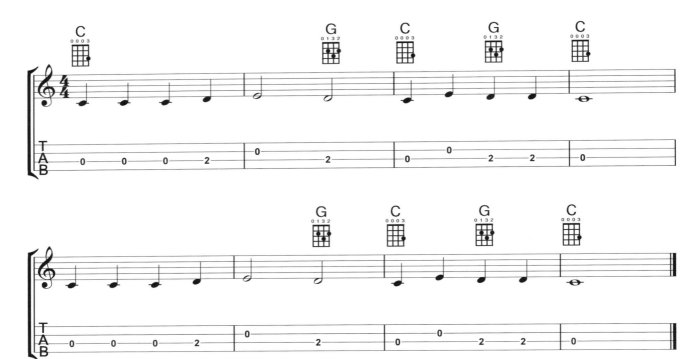

Swing Low, Sweet Chariot

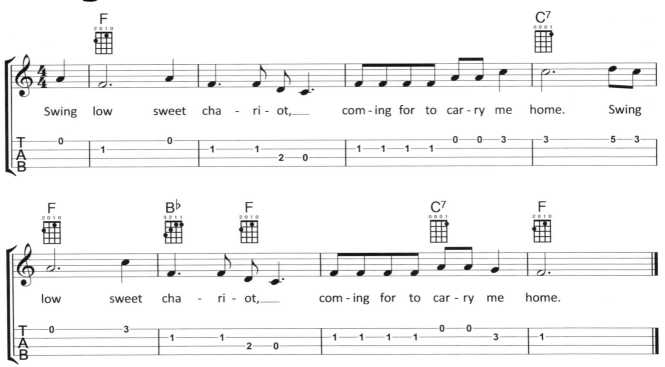

Kumbaya

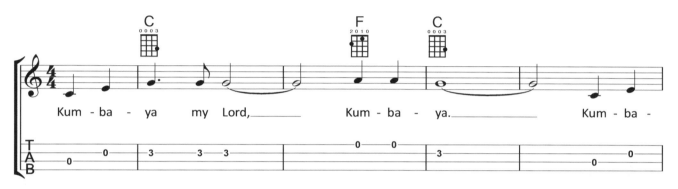

Kum - ba - ya my Lord, Kum - ba - ya. Kum - ba -

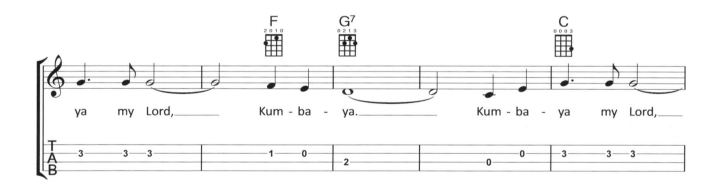

ya my Lord, Kum - ba - ya. Kum - ba - ya my Lord,

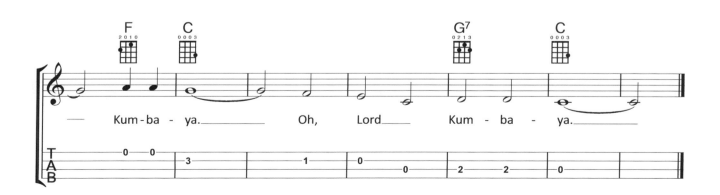

— Kum - ba - ya. Oh, Lord Kum - ba - ya.

Streets Of Laredo

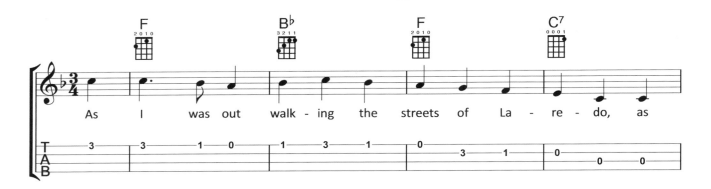

As I was out walk - ing the streets of La - re - do, as

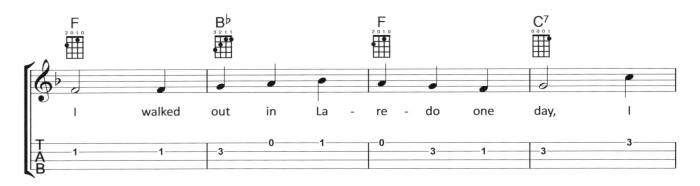

I walked out in La - re - do one day, I

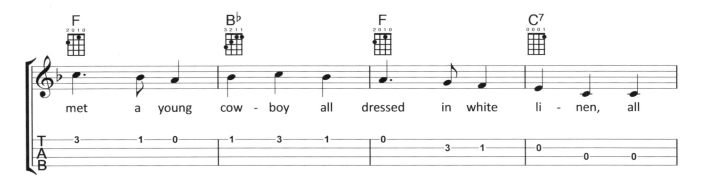

met a young cow - boy all dressed in white li - nen, all

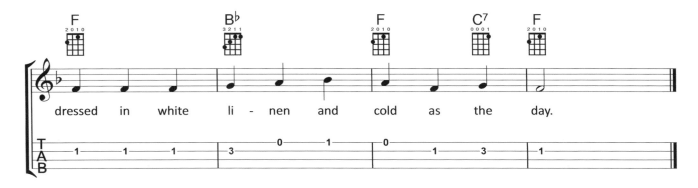

dressed in white li - nen and cold as the day.

Silent Night

Si - lent night, ho - ly night. All is calm,

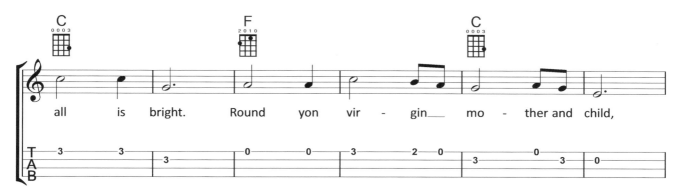

all is bright. Round yon vir - gin__ mo - ther and child,

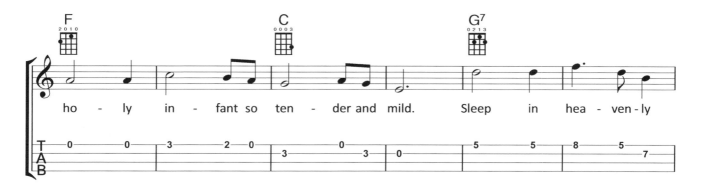

ho - ly in - fant so ten - der and mild. Sleep in hea - ven - ly

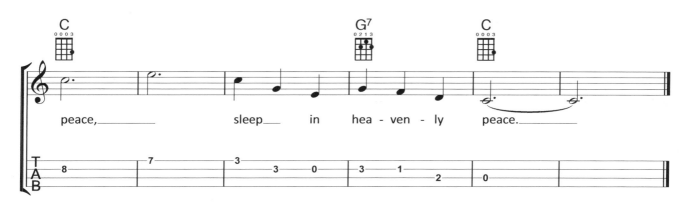

peace,____ sleep__ in hea - ven - ly peace.____

Oh, Susanna

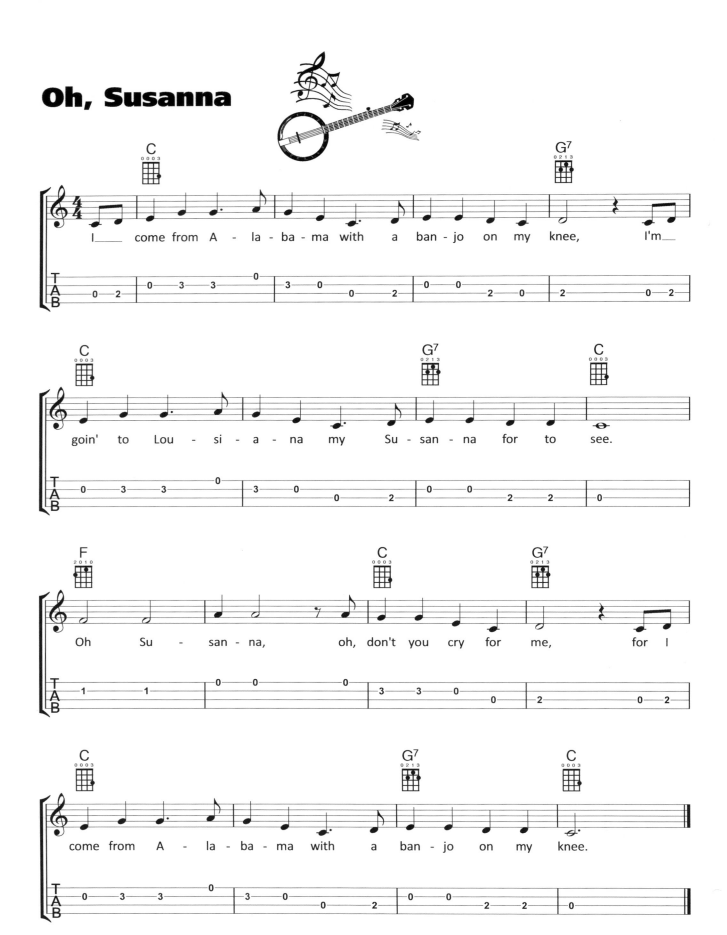

Ode To Joy

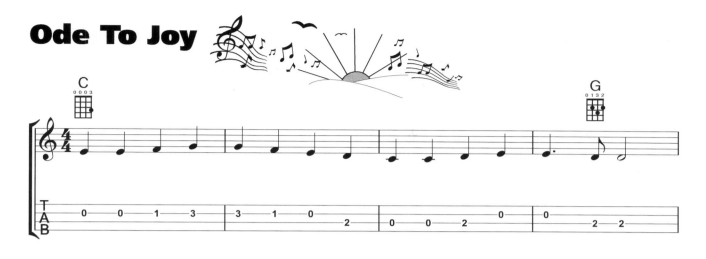

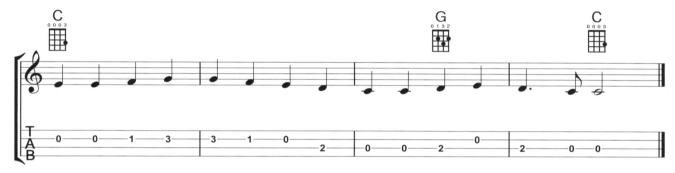

Drink To Me Only

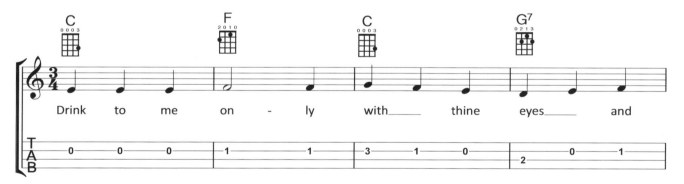

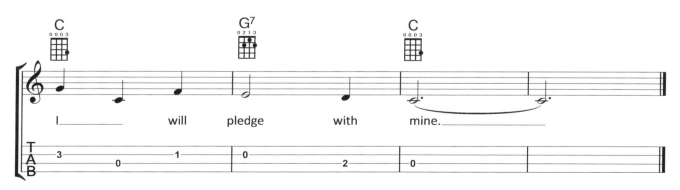

We Wish You A Merry Christmas

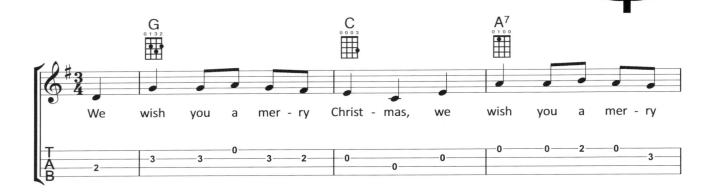

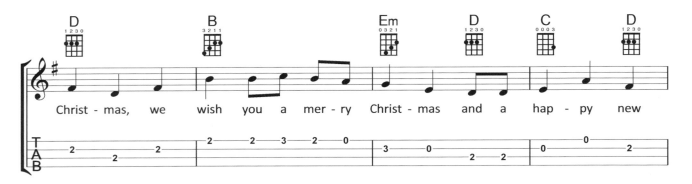

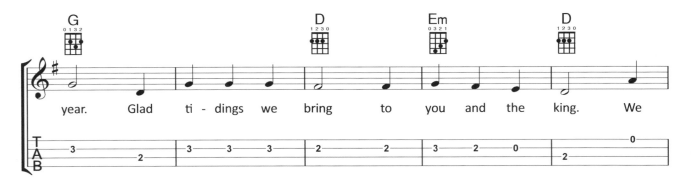

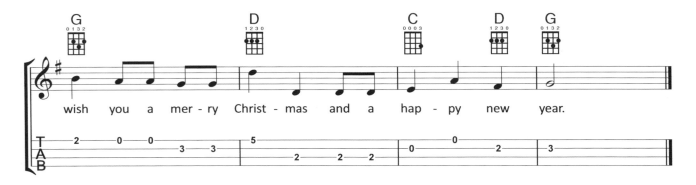

Oh Little Town Of Bethlehem

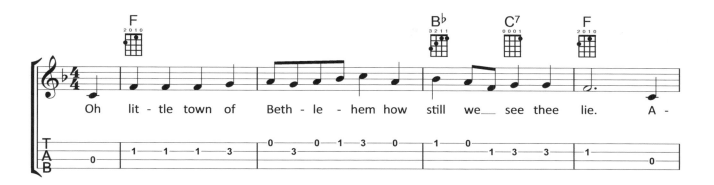

Oh lit - tle town of Beth - le - hem how still we__ see thee lie. A -

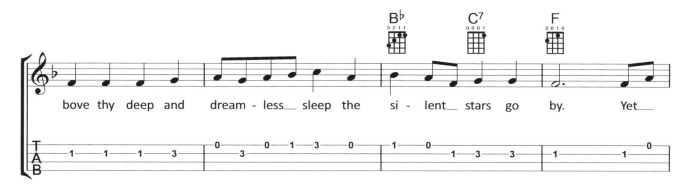

bove thy deep and dream - less__ sleep the si - lent__ stars go by. Yet__

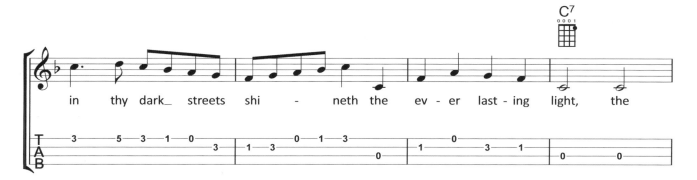

in thy dark__ streets shi - neth the ev - er last - ing light, the

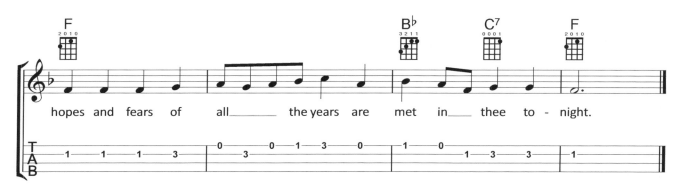

hopes and fears of all_____ the years are met in___ thee to - night.

Good King Wenceslas

We Three Kings Of Orient Are

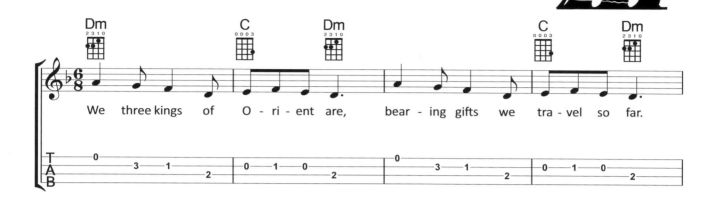

We three kings of O - ri - ent are, bear - ing gifts we tra - vel so far.

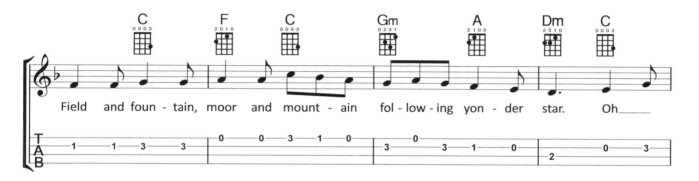

Field and foun - tain, moor and mount - ain fol - low - ing yon - der star. Oh_____

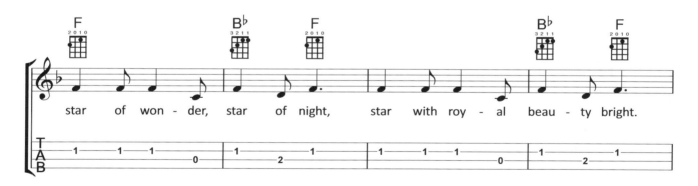

star of won - der, star of night, star with roy - al beau - ty bright.

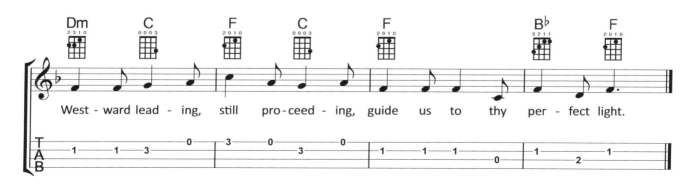

West - ward lead - ing, still pro - ceed - ing, guide us to thy per - fect light.

Jingle Bells

MORE GREAT MUSIC BOOKS FROM KYLE CRAIG!

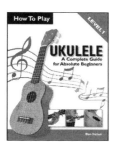

How To Play UKULELE — A Complete Guide for Absolute Beginners

978-1-908-707-08-6

My First UKULELE — Learn to Play: Kids

978-1-908-707-11-6

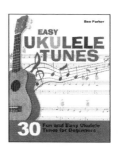

Easy UKULELE Tunes

978-1-908707-37-6

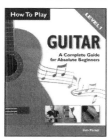

How To Play GUITAR — A Complete Guide for Absolute Beginners

978-1-908-707-09-3

My First GUITAR — Learn to Play: Kids

978-1-908-707-13-0

Easy GUITAR Tunes

978-1-908707-34-5

How To Play KEYBOARD — A Complete Guide for Absolute Beginners

978-1-908-707-14-7

My First KEYBOARD — Learn to Play: Kids

978-1-908-707-15-4

Easy KEYBOARD Tunes

978-1-908707-35-2

How To Play PIANO — A Complete Guide for Absolute Beginners

978-1-908-707-16-1

My First PIANO — Learn to Play: Kids

978-1-908-707-17-8

Easy PIANO Tunes

978-1-908707-33-8

How To Play HARMONICA — A Complete Guide for Absolute Beginners

978-1-908-707-28-4

My First RECORDER — Learn to Play: Kids

978-1-908-707-18-5

Easy RECORDER Tunes

978-1-908707-36-9

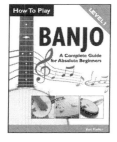

How To Play BANJO — A Complete Guide for Absolute Beginners

978-1-908-707-19-2

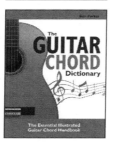

The GUITAR Chord Dictionary

978-1-908707-39-0

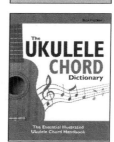

The UKULELE Chord Dictionary

978-1-908707-38-3

Printed in Great Britain
by Amazon